Mind over Monday

Your Mondays are…possible

Ashley D. Dawson

Dedication

I dedicate this book to God for breathing
life into this book to share with you. I also
dedicate this book to my grandmother,
Johnnie B. Dawson, as well as late mother
and grandfather, Jacqueline L. Dawson and
Clifford B. Dawson, for always believing in
me when I didn't even know how great I
really was. Lastly, I dedicate this book to all
my family and friends who push me to my
fullest potential and won't let me settle for
anything less. Love you always. ~ Daws

M&Ms Contents

Introduction

There's something about Mondays that many of us dread. It's almost like it's this daunting day we already tell ourselves to dread. Oftentimes it's our mindset about the day, thus setting our trajectory for the week. I'm not oblivious to life's happenings, and I know we will have our moments. What I'm talking about is that feeling you have for no reason on Mondays. I'm talking about that feeling when you automatically write the whole day off before it starts. Does any of this sound familiar, "Ugh, another Monday." "I already see how this day is gonna go." "I hate Mondays." Sound about right? Trust me, I overstand. There have been many Mondays where I've been exactly where you are right now, so many Mondays of sitting in the car and breaking down. At times it feels like all Mondays are the same. But are they really, or is our mindset always the same every Monday? Take a moment to really process that question. Yes, a Monday is a Monday, but the truth is, every day is a new day. If you agree with that statement, let me throw this at you. Every Monday is a new Monday.

Now that you've got your mind right (*LOL*), let me give you some context about the book. In 2018, I started writing and sharing positive messages at work. Every Monday, I would send a message titled, "M&M" which I would call "Monday Motivations." What started out as these quick positive notes evolved into positive messages. I've found that writing and sharing these messages have helped me and others change mindsets about Mondays. I'm inspired when writing these messages from various things (movies, songs, and life in general). They are meant to provoke thought, and I always leave off with a mental exercise (reflection for the week). Remember, we are setting our trajectory for the week. We are setting the direction of how we declare our week will go. Sharing these messages with colleagues isn't enough. Everyone needs inspiration, which is what you see before your eyes now. You will find weekly messages to jumpstart your Mondays, along with an opportunity for journaling. You must have a positive mindset over Mondays because your Mondays are POSSIBLE!!!

Each week will include the following:

- Weekly Affirmation

- M&M (Monday Motivation)

- Mental Exercise: Point to reflect on

- Soul-Search Saturday (Reflection for the week)

  - Glows: What went well for the week?

- Grows: What were the challenges for the week?

- Next Steps: What needs to happen for next week to be better?

WEEK 1:

RepotYourLife

Weekly Affirmation: **I am more than enough. I am worthy. I have a purpose. I make good choices. I choose to be better. I am better. I choose to have a great week on purpose!**

I'll admit planting is definitely not my thing, but I do know there are times you have to repot a plant. Do you know why? Repotting plants can restore life in the plant. As plants grow larger, the soil begins to decrease. The space for them to grow also decreases. As you can imagine, when this takes place, the plants won't thrive. They may begin to droop or not look as vibrant as they once did. This is a sign to find them a bigger pot so they can spread their roots. This is very similar to life. There are times when you just outgrow the pot you're in. You try to do what you can, but there's only so much soil. There's only so much growing you can do in your current pot before you begin to suffocate. Now you find yourself looking tired, unfulfilled, not happy, etc. That's a sign that it's time to pray for a new pot so that your roots can spread. It's time to grow and put some life back in yourself.

Have a great week on purpose!

Mental Exercise: Don't continue suffocating in the cramped pot. Repot your life and watch how you grow!

Soul-Search Saturday:

Glow(s):

_____

_____

_____

Grow(s)

_____

Next Steps:

_____

WEEK 2:

Focused

Weekly Affirmation: **I am more than enough. I am worthy. I have a purpose. I make good choices. I choose to be better. I am better. I choose to have a great week on purpose!**

While exercising one day and working on isolated leg movements, I was struggling to keep my balance. My sister told me, "take your time and focus on one point." When I took her advice, I began to keep my balance more and complete the exercise. Taking my time and focusing on that point helped me because what I was doing before was wobbling, trying to rush, and getting distracted by everything around me.

That's what life is like. When we have a mission, the enemy tricks us into thinking we have to rush to do it, and he throws everything at once to distract us. We have to take our time and focus. What God has for us is for us, so we don't have to rush. When God becomes the focal point, everything else will line up.

Mental Exercise: Take your time and focus on one point!

Have a great week on purpose!

Soul-Search Saturday:

Glow(s):

_____

_____

Grow(s)

_____

_____

_____

Next Steps:

_____

_____

_____

WEEK 3:

Adversity

Weekly Affirmation: **I am more than enough. I am worthy. I have a purpose. I make good choices. I choose to be better. I am better. I choose to have a great week on purpose!**

As a self-proclaimed popcorn connoisseur, I enjoy different types of popcorn. I decided to make some stovetop popcorn one day, as I'd always seen it and had been talking to a friend about it. She made some for her family, and I told her I was going to try it. Since it was my first time, I carefully followed the instructions. The process was so fascinating to me (*I have a thing about watching nothing turn into something*). As I was watching the kernels pop, something dawned on me. Kernels will only pop in heat. There are times in our life where we need to experience heat in order to pop to our fullest potential.

Mental Exercise: Don't be afraid of adversity because that's where the magic happens.

Have a great week on purpose!

Soul-Search Saturday:

Glow(s):

_____

_____

_____

Grow(s)

_____

_____

_____

Next Steps:

_____

_____

WEEK 4:

~

NewShoes

Weekly Affirmation: **I am more than enough. I am worthy. I have a purpose. I make good choices. I choose to be better. I am better. I choose to have a great week on purpose!**

Think back to when you were still growing or even a time when your current pair of shoes didn't fit anymore. Didn't they do you more harm than good? Did you still try to wear shoes that didn't fit? How far did you get in shoes that didn't fit? Am I right in saying that the best solution for you and your feet was to have a new pair of shoes? Let's think about this for a moment because we can compare this analogy to our own lives. Have you outgrown some people and situations? Are there people and situations doing you more harm than good right now? Are you still trying to wear something that doesn't fit? How far are you going to get trying to wear something that doesn't fit you anymore? Let's get back to the basics and just accept that it's time for new situations and new people. There's nothing wrong with the old, just as nothing was wrong with the old shoes… they just didn't fit anymore. Just like we had to part with our old shoes, you're going to have to keep away from the old people and old situations.

Mental Exercise: Let it go and stop trying to wear something that no longer fits. You've outgrown your shoes, and it's time for a new pair!

Have a great week on purpose!

Soul-Search Saturday:

Glow(s):

_____

_____

_____

Grow(s)

_____

_____

_____

Next Steps:

_____

_____

_____

WEEK 5:

Climb

Weekly Affirmation: **I am more than enough. I am worthy. I have a purpose. I make good choices. I choose to be better. I am better. I choose to have a great week on purpose!**

Occasionally I enjoy hiking up Stone Mountain. It's always a great workout that will push you mentally and physically. Whenever I climb, three major keys come to mind:

1. Everyone has a different pace. Some will be at the top waiting, and others will be climbing. Find YOUR pace.

2. There will be dips and challenges along the way. So what, keep pushing.

3. The only way to the top is consistently putting one foot in front of the other. Sometimes we stumble back, and sometimes we need a break. But never quit on yourself.

Mental Exercise: Anyone can stare and wish, but it takes courage to continue pushing and climbing to the top. You can do it!

Have a great week on purpose!

Soul-Search Saturday:

Glow(s):

_____

_____

_____

Grow(s)

_____

_____

_____

Next Steps:

_____

_____

_____

WEEK 6:

Survivor

Weekly Affirmation: **I am more than enough. I am worthy. I have a purpose. I make good choices. I choose to be better. I am better. I choose to have a great week on purpose!**

Take 30 seconds to reflect on your life, and I'm sure the following statements are true:

- You've beaten the odds

- You've displayed great courage AND strength

- You're a true inspiration

Guess what that makes you? A SURVIVOR!!! We are survivors!!!

Mental Exercise: Reflect on a time in your life that you've survived. You're stronger than you think.

Have a great week on purpose!

Soul-Search Saturday:

Glow(s):

_____

_____

_____

Grow(s)

_____

_____

_____

Next Steps:

_____

_____

_____

WEEK 7:

GetUp

Weekly Affirmation: **I am more than enough. I am worthy. I have a purpose. I make good choices. I choose to be better. I am better. I choose to have a great week on purpose!**

One night while watching TV, I caught the last few moments of the 1990 Douglas vs. Tyson fight. I'd heard about the fight, seen clips before, and heard Eric Thomas (motivational speaker) speak about the fight. But actually watching it was a different experience. The odds were 42-1, and Douglas was even knocked down in the 8th round. Many thought it was over and Tyson would remain the heavyweight champion of the world. Douglas may have even questioned if he could win the fight himself. But something great happened in the 10th round...Douglas knocked out the undefeated heavyweight champion Tyson!!!

Many may have counted you out. The odds may be stacked against you, and you may be the underdog; but the 10th round is here!!! The knockout is coming!!!

Mental Exercise: Get up and keep fighting because you are about to change the game.

Have a great week on purpose!

Soul-Search Saturday:

Glow(s):

_____

_____

_____

Grow(s)

_____

_____

Next Steps:

_____

WEEK 8:

Layover

Weekly Affirmation: **I am more than enough. I am worthy. I have a purpose. I make good choices. I choose to be better. I am better. I choose to have a great week on purpose!**

One of the things people either love or hate about flying is layovers. It's one of the things that people look at when booking flights. Also, it impacts the pricing of the flight. Some people want a shorter wait time so they can get to their next destination quicker. Some prefer a longer wait time, so they have time to move at their pace before their next flight. I prefer the latter. Of course, there are instances where we need to get somewhere quick, but if I don't, I prefer to travel at my pace these days. Regardless of which you prefer, a few things are synonymous with both:

- You must exit one plane and load another to get to your destination

- There will be a wait (short or long) before continuing on the journey

- Delays could potentially occur

We are all on a journey, but many people don't want to exit the plane they're on. You must exit the plane and load another to get to your next destination. Some people's layovers are shorter, and some are longer; either way, we have to learn patience. We must effectively utilize our time during layovers in life. Take time to check the itinerary to see if there have been any changes. Take time to gather yourself. Just like when flying, we may experience delays along the way. Embrace those and never rush the process. There's always a reason for a delay. No matter how late you think you'll get somewhere, you are right on schedule and where you should be at this moment in time.

Mental Exercise: Reflect on how you're handling the layover on this journey called life. Embrace the delays.

Have a great week on purpose!

Soul-Search Saturday:

Glow(s):

_____

_____

_____

Grow(s)

_____

_____

Next Steps:

_____

_____

WEEK 9:

LunarImpact

Weekly Affirmation: **I am more than enough. I am worthy. I have a purpose. I make good choices. I choose to be better. I am better. I choose to have a great week on purpose!**

I have to admit that competitive shows that test the mental and physical strength of contestants is one of my guilty pleasures. There's a show called "The Titan Games," which is one of my favorites. During one episode, there was a challenge called "Lunar Impact," where two contestants had to force each other off a platform that was 30 feet in the air. The challenge was like a mini suspense movie. Just when you thought one contestant would win, the other contestant made a major comeback. I encourage you to check out the video for this episode online. You'll walk away with three major keys:

1. Focus on the possibilities and not the reality

2. Never lose your drive

3. Push through the pain because that, in fact, is where your true strength is hidden

Mental Exercise: Never let anyone, not even yourself, count you out. Keep moving. Keep pushing. There's still time for you to come out victorious.

Have a great week on purpose!

Soul-Search Saturday:

Glow(s):

_____

_____

Grow(s)

_____

_____

Next Steps:

_____

_____

_____

Have a great week on purpose.

WEEK 10:

For You

Weekly Affirmation: **I am more than enough. I am worthy. I have a purpose. I make good choices. I choose to be better. I am better. I choose to have a great week on purpose!**

Dr. Steve Mariboli once said, "Every time I thought I was being rejected from something good, I was actually being redirected to something better." What's meant for you is for YOU. Learning, accepting, and believing this concept comes through some pain and struggle. It is through the pain and struggle that we actually grow and prepare for the redirection. Remember, there's no one like YOU.

Mental Exercise: "My heart is at ease knowing that what was meant for me will never miss me, and that what misses was never meant for me" ~Al-Shafii

Have a great week on purpose!

Soul-Search Saturday:

Glow(s):

_____

_____

_____

Grow(s)

_____

_____

Next Steps:

_____

_____

WEEK 11:

Adjust Your Focus

Weekly Affirmation: **I am more than enough. I am worthy. I have a purpose. I make good choices. I choose to be better. I am better. I choose to have a great week on purpose!**

Does life seem blurry right now? Do things seem out of balance? I can recall many times where my vision seemed a little off. Whenever this happened, I knew it was time to schedule an eye exam. After a few adjustments, my vision comes back into focus. May I direct your attention back to my opening question? There are times when life seems just a little off. It is in those moments where we need to adjust our focus.

Mental Exercise: What do you need to adjust in your life right now to get back in focus?

Have a great week on purpose!

Soul-Search Saturday:

Glow(s):

_____

_____

_____

Grow(s)

_____

_____

_____

Next Steps:

_____

_____

_____

WEEK 12:

Integrity

Weekly Affirmation: **I am more than enough. I am worthy. I have a purpose. I make good choices. I choose to be better. I am better. I choose to have a great week on purpose!**

It is often said that actions speak louder than words. I am a firm believer in this thought. To me, words come and go, but actions truly speak. I challenge us all to examine ourselves and HONESTLY answer the following questions:

- Do my actions line up with my words?

35

- Am I a person of integrity?

If you find the answers to be unfavorable, well, there's no better time than now to make a change.

Mental Exercise: What type of person are you when no one is watching?

Have a great week on purpose!

Soul-Search Saturday:

Glow(s):

_____

_____

_____

Grow(s)

_____

_____

Next Steps:

_____

_____

_____

WEEK 13:

BounceBack

Weekly Affirmation: **I am more than enough. I am worthy. I have a purpose. I make good choices. I choose to be better. I am better. I choose to have a great week on purpose!**

I'm sure many of us had our eyes glued to the TV in 2019 as we watched Tiger Woods win his 5th *Masters* title. We watched him come back from behind, stroke after stroke. No matter what the leaderboard said or how it fluctuated, Tiger just kept playing his game. We can learn a few things from Tiger's major comeback:

- Forget what the leaderboard says because it can change

- Our past does not define our future

- There will always be naysayers, whether we are up or down

- Remain calm and stay in the game

- Celebrate all victories, big and small

If you're down on the leaderboard, don't fret, because the game isn't over yet. I'll leave you with a line from one of my favorite Big Sean songs, "Last night took an L, but tonight I bounce back."

Mental Exercise: It's your time! Bounce back!!!

Have a great week on purpose!

Soul-Search Saturday:

Glow(s):

_____

_____

_____

Grow(s)

_____

_____

Next Steps:

_____

_____

_____

WEEK 14:

Originality

Weekly Affirmation: **I am more than enough. I am worthy. I have a purpose. I make good choices. I choose to be better. I am better. I choose to have a great week on purpose!**

When Popeye's debuted their chicken sandwich for the second time, it sparked a debate about who had the best chicken sandwich. Many people have claimed that Popeye's nailed it with their new sandwich, particularly the spicy version. Others have said, no, Chick-fil-A is still the best. There was even some Twitter beef, mostly between Popeye's and Wendy's. Chick-fil-A had one response to it all, "Bun + Chicken + Pickles = all the love for the original." The most powerful word was "original." Imitators argue and compare, but originals just sit back and continue doing what they've always done...be themselves. Many people may try to imitate what you do. They may very well get some fans, but the reality is you are the only original you. No one can do you better than you. People may have a recipe, but you will always have the special ingredient!

Mental Exercise: Celebrate your originality. Think about what makes you uniquely you.

Have a great week on purpose!

Soul-Search Saturday:

Glow(s):

_____

_____

_____

Grow(s)

_____

_____

Next Steps:

_____

_____

_____

WEEK 15:

Teamwork

Weekly Affirmation: **I am more than enough.
I am worthy. I have a purpose. I make good
choices. I choose to be better. I am better. I choose to
have a great week on purpose!**

I'm a sports enthusiast, but I have to admit, football is
my favorite time of the season. No shade to the other
sports, though. I really love them all. Whatever your favorite sport or team is, they all have one thing in common—teamwork. The funny thing about teamwork is
everyone has to know their role and be comfortable in
their role...whether in the game or on the sidelines. If

your time is on the sidelines, you can still be at your best and there for those in the game.

I recall a time when I went to a cookout. I was playing a card game with a few people, and it began to get dark (we were outside). I'd decided that I wasn't going to play anymore, but I'd watch instead. I also noticed that since it was getting dark, maybe those still playing could play better if I provided some light for them to see the cards. So, until everyone stopped playing, I designated myself as the person who would provide light so they could be at their best. I held the phone flashlight up with pride and enjoyed giving something that could help others. At one point, another person decided to shine their light too (Your light is contagious). I also was learning more about the game as I observed others. What are you going to do in the space you're in right now? When you're in the game, you know your role; but what if you are on the sidelines at the moment? Will you still give your all, but in a different capacity? What can you learn by observing others? How can you be the light to help someone else be more effective?

Mental Exercise: How can you be a better team member this week?

Have a great week on purpose!

Soul-Search Saturday:

Glow(s):

_____

_____

_____

Grow(s)

_____

_____

Next Steps:

_____

_____

WEEK 16:

Vulnerability

Weekly Affirmation: **I am more than enough. I am worthy. I have a purpose. I make good choices. I choose to be better. I am better. I choose to have a great week on purpose!**

Back in 2019, many of us watched Serena Williams fall short at the U.S. Open. What inspired me most was Serena's response to her loss. She didn't blame anyone, and she didn't make excuses. She acknowledged that she should have done better at that level and could have done better. That place of vulnerability is a game-changer. When you reach a certain level, being less than what you know you're capable of is unacceptable. We all experience bad days and have been off our game, but do we look at ourselves or others? Can we be vulnerable enough to admit our shortcomings? Can we hold ourselves accountable, or does accountability only apply to the next person?

Lastly, Serena didn't discount the talent of her opponent and admitted how Bianca puts pressure on her. There will always be new talent, but don't be intimidated. We should always stay on our toes and welcome the pressure. For that is where change takes place.

Mental Exercise: Perform at the level you know you are capable of and hold yourself accountable. Observe someone who keeps you on your toes and learn something new.

Have a great week on purpose!

Soul-Search Saturday:

Glow(s):

_____

_____

_____

Grow(s)

_____

_____

Next Steps:

_____

_____

_____

_____

WEEK 17:

AboveMeNow

Weekly Affirmation: **I am more than enough. I am worthy. I have a purpose. I make good choices. I choose to be better. I am better. I choose to have a great week on purpose!**

I love to have the window seat because I can get lost just by gazing at the clouds. When flying, I always notice the clouds. They look like small pillows from where we are. When we are looking up from ground level, the clouds look so huge; but when you are in the air, those same clouds look so small. This is our perspective about problems in comparison to God's perspective. When we are in the midst of it all and focusing on the problem, it looks so big. God sees all and above our problems. What looks big to us is minute to God. God sees the whole picture from His view, while we are just focused on one scene. It's above us now. This was a popular phrase from one of the Exonerated Five in Ava Duvernay's "When They See Us." This is a powerful statement because whatever we are facing is truly above us and in God's hands, if we CHOOSE to release it to Him. Drake said it best, "These days, I'm letting God handle all things above me!"

Mental Exercise: Relinquish control and give it to God.

Have a great week on purpose!

Soul-Search Saturday:

Glow(s):

_____

_____

_____

Grow(s)

_____

_____

_____

Next Steps:

_____

_____

_____

WEEK 18:

UpgradeLoading

Weekly Affirmation: **I am more than enough. I am worthy. I have a purpose. I make good choices. I choose to be better. I am better. I choose to have a great week on purpose!**

One summer, I was headed to San Francisco for a conference, and my aunt accompanied me on the trip. She required wheelchair assistance to maneuver around Atlanta's vast airport. As we were waiting at our gate to board, her transporter escorted us to the plane. As we were heading to the plane, the transporter told us that they had changed our seats to move us closer to the front. We didn't think anything of it. Our seats were originally 18D and 18E, so we figured they moved us up a few seats. We arrived at our new seats, 10B and 10C. As we sat down, we started looking around, and I noticed these were the Delta Comfort+ seats. There are various flight classes with Delta Airlines that range from First Class to Basic Economy. Once we got situated in the seats, I told my aunt they upgraded us from our Main Cabin seats to Comfort+ seats. We begin to notice the difference with the spacing, padded seat belts, padded seat pillow, and more legroom. Our particular seats were directly behind First Class, so we could see all the amenities they received. You don't hear me. We were going on the plane as planned, and we were surprisingly upgraded so we could be closer to the front. We were placed right behind the highest flight class on a plane.

You may be thinking it was just a move so my aunt could get off the plane sooner since she had wheelchair assistance. Perhaps, but may I present this to you? I had a trip the month before with wheelchair assistance, and I was in my same seat, which was actually on the LAST row of the plane. On that flight, I was in the back, right next to the bathroom. May I also drop this in your soul? We can be in the very back, absolutely last, in a situation that isn't the most pleasant, but God! God can upgrade your situation just like that. You may not be all the way in the front…yet, but He will show you what's coming by giving you a view of the next upgrade!!! So, was it just a move to accommodate my aunt? No, it was that and more. It was confirmation that God is doing some behind-the-scenes action to upgrade my situation.

Mental Exercise: If you're reading this, this is confirmation for your situation as well. Greater is coming. You're headed to First Class! Get ready!!!

Have a great week on purpose!

Soul-Search Saturday:

Glow(s):

_____

_____

_____

Grow(s)

_____

Next Steps:

_____

WEEK 19:

Attitude

Weekly Affirmation: **I am more than enough. I am worthy. I have a purpose. I make good choices. I choose to be better. I am better. I choose to have a great week on purpose!**

I remember a time where I struggled for weeks with my garage door opener. Each time I struggled, I told myself, "Daws, just get a new battery." I told myself that but kept putting it off. That worked, until it didn't. One particular day, I came home and could not get the garage door to open. I'd just gotten groceries and needed to get them in the house. You can imagine how upset

I was. I was mostly upset with myself because I'd said I was going to get a battery when I struggled leaving earlier that day, and I didn't. I called my sister, and she calmed me down and told me, go get a battery and come back to try the door again. I went to get a battery, changed it out, and tried again. This time there was no struggle, and the door opened. I could have saved myself a lot of time, frustration, and avoided messing the opener up by just changing the battery.

The point of this story is, there are things that are truly for us. This was my house and my garage, so I knew the garage should open. But all that didn't matter until I changed that battery. I truly believe that what's for us is for us, but attitude is EVERYTHING. A "dead" attitude can cause us to struggle, get frustrated, and even be costly at times. Many times we will continue going on, knowing that we need to change our attitude. There will come a point where that won't work anymore, and we are forced to change.

Mental Exercise: Look into yourselves and address areas where you need to change your batteries (*attitude*); then make a decision to do so immediately.

Have a great week on purpose!

Soul-Search Saturday:

Glow(s):

_____

_____

_____

Grow(s)

_____

Next Steps:

_____

WEEK 20:

Connectivity

Weekly Affirmation: **I am more than enough. I am worthy. I have a purpose. I make good choices. I choose to be better. I am better. I choose to have a great week on purpose!**

I can remember how I loved playing *Connect Four* as a child. There was something exciting about going back and forth with your opponent as you tried to connect four of your color discs. The winner was the first person to connect four of their discs in a horizontal, vertical, or diagonal line. We all represent a disc, and when we're connected, we all win. This is a simple, yet powerful message.

Mental Exercise: Get connected.

Have a great week on purpose!

Soul-Search Saturday:

Glow(s):

_____

_____

_____

Grow(s)

_____

_____

_____

Next Steps:

_____

_____

_____

WEEK 21:

Expansion

Weekly Affirmation: **I am more than enough. I am worthy. I have a purpose. I make good choices. I choose to be better. I am better. I choose to have a great week on purpose!**

When I go to the grocery store, I'm amazed when I walk down the cereal aisle. I pride myself on being a cereal connoisseur, but this definitely surprised me. I counted 14, yes 14, different varieties of *Cheerios* from original to chocolate peanut butter. In the business world, this is called product expansion. During a company's life cycle, they will upgrade existing products or

65

develop new products. Some reasons for product expansion are:

- More market opportunities

- Changing customer needs

- Increase customer loyalty

Someone once told me that we are our own business and should act as such. If this is the case, shouldn't we expand as well during our life cycle? Just like a company, we must expand to open ourselves to more opportunities, respond to customer needs, and increase our customer loyalty.

Mental Exercise: Write down one way you plan to expand yourself.

Have a great week on purpose!

Soul-Search Saturday:

Glow(s):

_____

_____

_____

Grow(s)

_____

_____

Next Steps:

_____

_____

WEEK 22:

Reset

Weekly Affirmation: **I am more than enough. I am worthy. I have a purpose. I make good choices. I choose to be better. I am better. I choose to have a great week on purpose!**

I'm sure you've seen "Reset to Factory Default Settings" on your phone. This reset will cause all software and settings to be reset, but personal content won't be deleted in the process. Sometimes we need to get back to the basics and "Reset to Factory Default Settings." We have to reset our thoughts (software) and our mindsets (settings). We don't have to lose ourselves (personal content) in the process, but we do need to reset at times.

Mental Exercise: Press the reset button.

Have a great week on purpose!

Soul-Search Saturday:

Glow(s):

_____

_____

_____

Grow(s)

_____

_____

_____

Next Steps:

_____

_____

_____

WEEK 23:

MoveDifferent

Weekly Affirmation: **I am more than enough. I am worthy. I have a purpose. I make good choices. I choose to be better. I am better. I choose to have a great week on purpose!**

Remember the Titans is one of my favorite movies. There are so many nuggets embedded in the movie. There is one particular scene where the football team is practicing, and the coach is telling them how they would change the way they do everything. I took four things away from that scene:

- We must change the way we move

- We have to be in rhythm with our movements

- Old mindsets won't take us to new destinations

- We are either all in or all out. The fence is full.

When Denzel says, "Come on, move those feet." I felt all of that. We have to move in rhythm so we **all** can eat.

Mental Exercise: If you want something different, you have to move differently.

Have a great week on purpose!

Soul-Search Saturday:

Glow(s):

_____

_____

_____

Grow(s)

_____

_____

Next Steps:

_____

_____

_____

WEEK 24:

OneBandOneSound

Weekly Affirmation: **I am more than enough. I am worthy. I have a purpose. I make good choices. I choose to be better. I am better. I choose to have a great week on purpose!**

"One band, one sound" was a very popular line and concept from the movie "Drumline." I believe we all need to be reminded of this from time to time. The other line that was most impactful to me was, "When one sounds bad, we <u>all</u> look and sound bad." Take a moment to think about a band playing and one instrument being off. Everyone notices and begins to talk about how that one instrument is throwing the sound off. What is the sound of a team when one person is off? Two people? You get the point. Yes, things happen, but this isn't about that. This is about taking personal feelings out of the equation and operating in excellence, regardless of the position or title.

Mental Exercise: Are you in tune? If not, make the necessary adjustment. One band. One sound.

Have a great week on purpose!

Soul-Search Saturday:

Glow(s):

_____

_____

Grow(s)

_____

_____

_____

Next Steps:

_____

_____

_____

WEEK 25:

EnjoyTheJourney

Weekly Affirmation: **I am more than enough. I am worthy. I have a purpose. I make good choices. I choose to be better. I am better. I choose to have a great week on purpose!**

I remember a time when I went out to eat with my aunt and grandmother. The line was super long when we arrived. We were dreading the wait, but my grandmother loves this restaurant, so we stayed. As I was waiting in line, I was growing impatient and hangry, but I focused on other things while waiting (decorations, people, etc.). As we got closer to the line to order, I looked back and noticed how far we had come. At that moment, I realized the lesson in all of it. There will be many times where we have to wait for things that we really want. We may dread it at first, but take time to enjoy the journey along the way.

Mental Exercise: Take some time to reflect on how far you've come. You may still have some ways to go, but you're definitely not where you started. Enjoy the journey.

Have a great week on purpose!

Soul-Search Saturday:

Glow(s):

_____

_____

_____

Grow(s)

_____

_____

Next Steps:

_____

_____

_____

WEEK 26:

Bloom

Weekly Affirmation: **I am more than enough. I am worthy. I have a purpose. I make good choices. I choose to be better. I am better. I choose to have a great week on purpose!**

There's one flower that piques my interest, and it's the Eureka Valley evening primrose. What makes this plant so rare is its ability to not only grow but also survive in a challenging and ever-changing environment. It grows on sand dunes in Death Valley National Park. Think about that last sentence for a moment. Like this rare plant, you too have bloomed in heated and uncommon environments. You reading this confirms that you have a purpose.

Mental Exercise: Keep blooming where you are. I would also encourage you to look up this flower. Its growth cycle is very interesting.

Have a great week on purpose!

Soul-Search Saturday:

Glow(s):

_____

_____

Grow(s)

_____

_____

_____

Next Steps:

_____

_____

_____

WEEK 27:

Lessons

Weekly Affirmation: **I am more than enough. I am worthy. I have a purpose. I make good choices. I choose to be better. I am better. I choose to have a great week on purpose!**

Educators teach students a lesson, then check for understanding of what they taught. This can be quick checks or opportunities for students to apply their learning. Whatever the method is, the expected end result is that students have digested the material and mastered a skill. If at any time this is found not to be the case, the lesson must be revisited. It can be frustrating because we want to move on, and the student does too, but what's a lesson without a skill that can't be applied in life? So, you feel me on that, right? Ok, hold that thought.

Through our journeys in life, we learn many lessons. We are also presented with many opportunities that check for our understanding, quick checks and application. Life is a classroom, and we are the students. We must digest the lessons taught and master a skill to apply in our lives. As students in this classroom of life, we often have lessons that must be revisited as well. Yes, we want to move on, but remember what we agreed on earlier. What's a lesson without a skill that can't be applied in life?

Mental Exercise: Learn the lesson. Master the skill.

Have a great week on purpose!

Soul-Search Saturday:

Glow(s):

_____

_____

_____

Grow(s)

_____

_____

Next Steps:

_____

_____

_____

WEEK 28:

Discipline

Weekly Affirmation: **I am more than enough. I am worthy. I have a purpose. I make good choices. I choose to be better. I am better. I choose to have a great week on purpose!**

Majority of the time, I'm locked in with nutrition and wellness because I want to stay healthy and treat my body well. Every now and then, I'll go to the store, and everything I don't need seems so tempting to buy. I can recall one time when I went to the store to get my meal prep items, and what did I see as soon as I walked in the door? My favorite brand of chips, Kettle, were

BOGO (Buy One, Get One) free. Not only were these literally in the area where the shopping carts were, but they were the cheapest I'd ever seen. They had my favorite flavor, Bourbon BBQ, and some others I hadn't tried. It was at this moment I had a choice to make. Was I going to stick to my discipline or give in and justify my actions with having done so well all month? I chose discipline because my why was stronger than a temporary decision. Was it hard? YES, because I LOVE those chips. But, being disciplined and consistent in my mission meant more to me at that moment. If we truly want to move to the next level, we have to be disciplined. The basic definition of discipline is to obey rules or a code of behavior. Discipline is a mindset. It's the manner in which we move, even in the midst of temptation. Discipline and consistency; that's what moves the needle.

Mental Exercise: What is one way you can be more disciplined and consistent?

Have a great week on purpose!

Soul-Search Saturday:

Glow(s):

_____

_____

Grow(s)

_____

_____

Next Steps:

_____

_____

_____

WEEK 29:

BiggerPicture

Weekly Affirmation: **I am more than enough. I am worthy. I have a purpose. I make good choices. I choose to be better. I am better. I choose to have a great week on purpose!**

When I was younger, I was always intrigued by puzzles. I loved taking individual pieces and putting them together to recreate the beautiful picture on the box. I can only imagine how frustrated I would have been if there would have been pieces missing. Every piece in that puzzle box was needed. Any missing piece would have thrown the whole picture off. We don't always see the bigger picture, but know that your individual puzzle piece is always needed for the bigger picture.

Mental Exercise: Don't ever discount your significance because you matter. Your puzzle piece is needed.

Have a great week on purpose!

Soul-Search Saturday:

Glow(s):

_____

_____

_____

Grow(s)

_____

_____

Next Steps:

_____

_____

_____

WEEK 30:

CheckEngine

Weekly Affirmation: **I am more than enough. I am worthy. I have a purpose. I make good choices. I choose to be better. I am better. I choose to have a great week on purpose!**

Many of us have seen the "check engine" symbol in a car, which alerts drivers that they should check out what's going on with their vehicle. This symbol can be a steady light, in which you should get your car checked as soon as possible. The symbol can also be a flashing light, in which you need to stop and get the vehicle checked immediately.

As you read this, you may have a personal "check engine" light on. You may even have a flashing light. Take a moment to assess where you are personally. You've had some signs, so let this be additional confirmation to STOP.

Mental Exercise: Give yourself permission to just be. Examine your engine and respond accordingly.

Have a great week on purpose!

Soul-Search Saturday:

Glow(s):

_____

_____

_____

Grow(s)

_____

_____

_____

Next Steps:

_____

_____

_____

WEEK 31:

MoveIt

Weekly Affirmation: **I am more than enough. I am worthy. I have a purpose. I make good choices. I choose to be better. I am better. I choose to have a great week on purpose!**

Take a moment to think about a car that's idle. It's not a good idea for cars to stay idle for too long because of issues that could potentially occur when the car isn't used regularly. Parts can begin to deteriorate and age prematurely. That same can be true with our bodies when we leave them idle for too long. Just like a car is meant to be driven, our bodies are meant to move.

Mental Exercise: Get moving, right where we are. This is the week to get it done!

Have a great week on purpose!

Soul-Search Saturday:

Glow(s):

_____

_____

_____

Grow(s)

_____

_____

_____

Next Steps:

_____

_____

_____

WEEK 32:

Transformation

Weekly Affirmation: **I am more than enough. I am worthy. I have a purpose. I make good choices. I choose to be better. I am better. I choose to have a great week on purpose!**

Butterflies are very intriguing, partly because of their process before becoming the beauty we see before our eyes. They begin as a caterpillar in which they eat everything, grow, and shed many times during this stage. The caterpillars then come to a point where they transform into a chrysalis or outer covering for the next transformation. It is during this stage that the caterpillar breaks down and begins to transform into a butterfly. Then, when the time is right, the butterfly emerges. The butterfly flaps its wings to dry them out and help blood flow through the wings. At this point, the butterfly is ready to take flight.

I think it's important for us to understand our stage of transformation. We go through each stage many times throughout our lives, but knowing where we are helps us to respond better. Are we a caterpillar? Should we be gaining all the knowledge we can and growing? Are we in a chrysalis? Should we be still and allow everything to break down so we can transform? Are we a butterfly? Should we be emerging? Should we be flapping our wings and preparing to take flight? Is it time to fly? Whatever stage in the process, all are useful and valuable to our growth.

Mental Exercise: What stage are you currently in? How will you respond differently?

Have a great week on purpose!

Soul-Search Saturday:

Glow(s):

_____

_____

Grow(s)

_____

_____

Next Steps:

_____

_____

_____

WEEK 33:

Detroit

Weekly Affirmation: **I am more than enough. I am worthy. I have a purpose. I make good choices. I choose to be better. I am better. I choose to have a great week on purpose!**

Like many of us, I thoroughly enjoyed watching the *The Last Dance* documentary. One of the most memorable points was about the challenges Chicago had in defeating Detroit during that time. It was interesting to hear about the Pistons and their "Bad Boys" from another perspective. The 1990 conference matchup between the two teams was most interesting. The Pistons ended the Bulls' chance at playing for their first championship once *again*. This made the third year in a row, and this loss was the final straw for the Bulls.

The Pistons were a very physical team, and the Bulls knew they had to make some adjustments if they wanted to defeat Detroit the following year. They decided instead of taking a vacation that summer, they would train. The team had to get tougher, and Michael Jordan, particularly, wanted to gain more muscle. Detroit had a whole set of rules for Michael Jordan, which was pretty much to stop him by any means necessary. Chicago knew their best chance at beating Detroit was to equip themselves to handle their physicality and get just as physical. *My question to you is, what or who is your "Detroit?"*

Mental Exercise: Identify the adjustments and sacrifices we need to make to defeat our "Detroit."

Have a great week on purpose!

This doesn't reflect on the city of Detroit at all. It's representative of challenges in your life. Detroit is a great city!

Soul-Search Saturday:

Glow(s):

_____

_____

_____

Grow(s)

_____

_____

_____

Next Steps:

_____

_____

_____

WEEK 34:

Layers

Weekly Affirmation: **I am more than enough. I am worthy. I have a purpose. I make good choices. I choose to be better. I am better. I choose to have a great week on purpose!**

What do polishing nails and applying eye makeup have in common? Well, there is one major key in both, which is building depth. My sister always says when you apply eye makeup, you have to build the depth. She says the key to a great look is starting out with a little and gradually building from there. Ever since she first said this, it really hit home. This is true when polishing nails as well. You don't start out with a lot because it will look clumpy, so you polish it in layers. We can apply this same concept to our life. We must be patient and gradually build, layer by layer.

Mental Exercise: I challenge you this week to take your time and apply in layers. The end result will be a smooth, polished, and natural look.

Have a great week on purpose!

Soul-Search Saturday:

Glow(s):

_____

_____

_____

Grow(s)

_____

Next Steps:

_____

WEEK 35:

ManageStorage

Weekly Affirmation: **I am more than enough. I am worthy. I have a purpose. I make good choices. I choose to be better. I am better. I choose to have a great week on purpose!**

I remember a time when I received an email stating that I was almost out of space on my iCloud. This was strange because I have the 50GB plan, which I've had for years, and I've never received this message. Of course, there was an offer to get more storage, but I was thinking I needed to identify the issue first. This prompted me to go to "manage storage" under my iCloud settings to see everything on the phone that was taking up storage. I was also able to see how much storage each item was taking up. I had some decisions to make. It was time to let some things go to free up space. I begin going down the list and deleting. The more I deleted, the more I saw my storage capacity move in the opposite direction. My next step was to purge my photos as well as the photos, attachments, and links within my text messages. When I did that, I was able to free up more space. There will be times, perhaps that time is now, where we need to check the "manage storage" settings in our lives and delete. We don't have to store everything.

Mental Exercise: Do an analysis of what's taking up space and delete that which doesn't align with your purpose anymore.

Have a great week on purpose!

Soul-Search Saturday:

Glow(s):

_____

_____

_____

Grow(s)

_____

_____

_____

Next Steps:

_____

_____

_____

WEEK 36:

GoneFishin

W eekly Affirmation: **I am more than enough. I am worthy. I have a purpose. I make good choices. I choose to be better. I am better. I choose to have a great week on purpose!**

I don't know too much about fishing, but I know it can be calming or frustrating, depending on your perception. I've also learned that many factors determine the best time to catch fish. The two conditions that are most interesting to me are: cloudy days and rising tides. These stand out because people often associate cloudy days as being gloomy and rising tides with a possible storm. The thing is, the cloudy days make the environment more comfortable for fish, improving your chances of catching more. Additionally, the rising tides move the water, thus moving the bait, which brings more fish out to catch.

The same can be true for our lives. Don't look at "cloudy" days as being the end or get stressed when the "tides" begin to rise. Those cloudy days and rising tides are creating a space for you to catch your blessings.

Mental Exercise: Grab your equipment, get ready, and let's go fishin'. You're about to catch your blessings!!!

Have a great week on purpose!

Soul-Search Saturday:

Glow(s):

_____

_____

_____

Grow(s)

_____

Next Steps:

_____

WEEK 37:

Change Your Filter

Weekly Affirmation: I am more than enough. I am worthy. I have a purpose. I make good choices. I choose to be better. I am better. I choose to have a great week on purpose!

It's very important to change the air filters in your home. Air filters are very important because they help our heating and cooling systems run efficiently; protect systems; keep dust from the building; and more importantly, save money and energy. When we don't change our filters as we should, we cause issues in our home, causing our systems to work harder. We won't get all the air/heat we need, making it less comfortable in our homes. This can also cause mold and bacteria to build up. When our systems work harder, they could potentially overheat or freeze, causing us to spend more money than necessary. We could end up having repairs that could be avoided by checking and changing the filter regularly.

Have you checked your internal filter lately? How's it looking? Just like with air filters, neglecting this check can cause us to work harder, cause negativity to build up, or cause us to break down. When there's build-up, we can't get all that we deserve. All of these can be costly. If you notice that you aren't operating at your best, it may be time to change your internal filter.

Mental Exercise: Is it time to change your internal filter? We can avoid many issues when we make the necessary assessments.

Have a great week on purpose!

Soul-Search Saturday:

Glow(s):

_____

_____

_____

Grow(s)

_____

_____

_____

Next Steps:

_____

_____

_____

WEEK 38:

Love Yourz

Weekly Affirmation: **I am more than enough. I am worthy. I have a purpose. I make good choices. I choose to be better. I am better. I choose to have a great week on purpose!**

J. Cole has a song titled, "Love Yourz" where he begins the song saying, "No such thing as a life that's better than yours…No such thing as a life that's better than yours…No such thing, no such thing." I loved this song from the moment I heard it because it really makes you think. Too often, we look at other people and think how much better their life may be. It's almost like riding through a neighborhood and looking at homes, thinking a home is better than your home. You look at the outside and may even look it up online to get a glimpse of the inside. The thing is, the outside can look great, and pictures online are meant to depict the house in the best way. We can't always go off what we see on the outside or what's posted online. This applies to a home or someone's life. The outside may look good, and what they post may look even better, but the true inside could be a mess. We have to learn to appreciate who we are and what we have because, like J. Cole said, "Love Yourz."

Mental Exercise: Love and appreciate the life you have. While you're wishing you had someone else's life, someone could be wishing for your life.

Have a great week on purpose!

Soul-Search Saturday:

Glow(s):

_____

_____

_____

Grow(s)

_____

Next Steps:

_____

WEEK 39:

Devotion

Weekly Affirmation: **I am more than enough. I am worthy. I have a purpose. I make good choices. I choose to be better. I am better. I choose to have a great week on purpose!**

Earth, Wind, & Fire was my mom's favorite group, and I can remember her playing their records repeatedly. One particular song I heard often was "Devotion," and I always wondered why she played it so much. Besides the therapeutic harmonies and smooth rhythm of the song, I believe it was also because of the meaning. It's funny how song lyrics have deeper meaning the more you've experienced life. During these times, everyone needs their spirits uplifted. There's so much pain, and if you're a feeler like me, it can become overwhelming at times. We must find those things that bring us peace, and we **must** protect our peace.

"In everyone's life, there's a need to be happy. Let the sun shine a smile your way. Open your heart, feel the touch of devotion. Maybe this song will help uplift your day. Make a better way" "Devotion" ~Earth, Wind, & Fire

Mental Exercise: What is your devotion?

Have a great week on purpose!

Soul-Search Saturday:

Glow(s):

_____

_____

Grow(s):

_____

_____

_____

Next Steps:

_____

_____

_____

WEEK 40:

Chosen

Weekly Affirmation: **I am more than enough. I am worthy. I have a purpose. I make good choices. I choose to be better. I am better. I choose to have a great week on purpose!**

I became a plant mom a few years back, and surprisingly my babies have taken my heart. I'm always looking to expand my family, so I'm always going to the nursery. I can recall one weekend I went to the nursery and saw a group of beautiful plants. The interesting colors (pink and green) lured me over. As I was trying to decide which one I wanted, there was one plant tucked away in the background. Even though this plant wasn't easily visible, there was something about this one that stood out. There were some imperfections, but that made it stand out more. Those imperfections gave it character and ignited something in me that said, "that's the one." There were others that some may have said were better to pick, but it was all about the connection for me.

Sometimes we are in the background, and you may be now, wondering if people notice you. Don't stop being who you are or try to fit the mold of others around you. Everything about you will be everything someone is looking for. There will be a connection and something about you that stands out from everyone else. There's something about you that will make someone say, "they're the one." If no one has told you lately, I see you!

Mental Exercise: Embrace all parts of who you are, even the imperfections.

Have a great week on purpose!

Soul-Search Saturday:

Glow(s):

_____

_____

_____

Grow(s)

_____

_____

Next Steps:

_____

WEEK 41:

Alright

Weekly Affirmation: **I am more than enough. I am worthy. I have a purpose. I make good choices. I choose to be better. I am better. I choose to have a great week on purpose!**

"Life can bring us through many changes. It's alright. Just don't give up, know that it's going to be alright."

Read those words again. This comes from one of my favorite songs by Ledisi. It's one of those feel-good songs you have to play on repeat at least three times. It's a reminder that everything will be alright. How do I know? I sat by mom's bedside at 18 years old as she took her last breath. I sat by my granddaddy's bedside as he took his last breath. I don't tell you this for sympathy; I tell you this because those were two of the worst days in my life, and I still find joy in each day. You have your own stories, and you may be in a valley experience right now, but it's going to be alright. You've survived 100% of your worst days. You're a survivor! We are survivors!!! Don't give up.

Mental Exercise: I challenge you to complete the sentence, "I'm alright because_____."

Have a great week on purpose!

Soul-Search Saturday:

Glow(s):

_____

_____

Grow(s)

_____

_____

Next Steps:

_____

_____

_____

WEEK 42:

StrengthTraining

Weekly Affirmation: **I am more than enough. I am worthy. I have a purpose. I make good choices. I choose to be better. I am better. I choose to have a great week on purpose!**

"Can you spot me?"

This is a phrase often heard when people are doing strength training. The spotter serves a few purposes:

- Makes sure you have proper form and don't injure yourself

- Keeps you focused on the goal

- Makes sure the weight doesn't injure you when you get tired from sets and/or heaviness of the weight

- Motivates you to push through

- Provides assistance when you get stuck so you can succeed

Isn't this life? At times we need a spot, and other times we need a spotter. There are times when we need feedback, motivation, and assistance. Then there are times when we need to do the same for someone else.

Mental Exercise: Embrace whatever side of the weight you currently find yourself.

Have a great week on purpose!

Soul-Search Saturday:

Glow(s):

_____

_____

_____

Grow(s)

_____

_____

_____

Next Steps:

_____

_____

_____

WEEK 43:

Focus

Weekly Affirmation: **I am more than enough. I am worthy. I have a purpose. I make good choices. I choose to be better. I am better. I choose to have a great week on purpose!**

I can remember when I played softball and basketball in high school. There was one thing in common for both that comes to mind, and that's "focus." In basketball, my coach drilled into us to follow through on our shot. In order to do this, we needed to be focused on what we were doing so we could respond accordingly. In softball, you definitely had to be focused on the ball.

When it came to hitting, you needed focus to determine whether to swing or not. On defense, it would behoove you to focus on the ball being hit if you didn't want to get hit by the ball. This was definitely the case in the infield because losing focus could cause you to get popped in the face. You have to focus and pay attention.

Mental Exercise: I challenge you this week to focus and pay attention to what you're doing and what's going on around you. Be in the moment.

Have a great week on purpose!

Soul-Search Saturday:

Glow(s):

_____

_____

_____

Grow(s):

_____

_____

_____

Next Steps:

_____

_____

_____

WEEK 44:

BeKind

Weekly Affirmation: **I am more than enough. I am worthy. I have a purpose. I make good choices. I choose to be better. I am better. I choose to have a great week on purpose!**

Many were stunned and saddened to hear the news of Chadwick Boseman's passing. There was so much talent and poise about him, but his strength is undeniable. For years he graciously shared his gifts and talents with the world while privately fighting his own battle. He pushed beyond limits even when his body may have been ridden with pain at times. His unselfish talent is truly what makes him a superhero. We must be kind to others because we never know the personal struggles they have. It's not our place to ration out kindness to those we think are deserving, but it is our place to be a kind person. Truth be told, we all have moments where we are undeserving, but someone was still kind to us.

Mental Exercise: I challenge you this week and forever more to be a kind person. Be a good human.

Have a great week on purpose!

Soul-Search Saturday:

Glow(s):

_____

_____

_____

Grow(s)

_____

_____

Next Steps:

_____

WEEK 45:

New View

Weekly Affirmation: **I am more than enough. I am worthy. I have a purpose. I make good choices. I choose to be better. I am better. I choose to have a great week on purpose!**

It's always interesting to watch my dog Ace, particularly at my grandparents' house. It's fascinating to watch him come into the house and how he always bypasses the ramp that's closest to the door. He goes all the way around to come up through the carport. I've had him nine years, so he knows the house well, and he knows about that ramp. At any rate, I'm sure he's accustomed to entering the house one way, but I always think he wouldn't have to work as hard if he just used the ramp. That's us sometimes though. We are so accustomed to doing something one way, focused on our way, that we totally bypass a more efficient way. That way can be right in our face, but we still choose to do things our way. Yes, our way can get the job done, but perhaps a new way can get it done better.

Mental Exercise: I challenge you to be open to new views.

Have a great week on purpose!

Soul-Search Saturday:

Glow(s):

_____

_____

_____

_____

Grow(s)

_____

_____

_____

Next Steps:

_____

_____

_____

WEEK 46:

SmallBeginnings

Weekly Affirmation: **I am more than enough. I am worthy. I have a purpose. I make good choices. I choose to be better. I am better. I choose to have a great week on purpose!**

People often discount small beginnings, but small drips can make big puddles. Don't believe me? Ask any ceiling that has a discolored stain from a small drip. I remember a time where I noticed a large area of discoloration on my ceiling, so I called a roofer to see what was going on. When they went into the attic, they found a small, slow drip that was running down and causing a puddle of water. Like I said, small drips can make big puddles.

Mental Exercise: Embrace small beginnings and keep dripping, because your presence will soon soak through.

Have a great week on purpose!

Soul-Search Saturday:

Glow(s):

_____

_____

_____

Grow(s)

_____

Next Steps:

_____

_____

WEEK 47:

BeReady

Weekly Affirmation: I am more than enough. I am worthy. I have a purpose. I make good choices. I choose to be better. I am better. I choose to have a great week on purpose!

About a year ago, my mailbox was knocked down by the sanitation company. As a result, I had to go by the post office to get my mail. When I arrived, I told them that I had received messages for two packages I was expecting. The messages told me that my packages were being held at the post office. When they brought my mail out, there was a note that read, "Box down,

10-day hold." Yes, the packages I was expecting were sent to me, but the mailbox wasn't up and ready to receive them.

Let me ask you this. Are you ready to receive the packages that you're expecting in your life? Are you up and ready to receive, or are you lying down while your packages are on hold? We should live with an attitude of great expectations, but we also have to be ready.

Mental Exercise: How do you need to prepare for what you're expecting?

Have a great week on purpose!

Soul-Search Saturday:

Glow(s):

_____

_____

Grow(s)

_____

_____

Next Steps:

_____

_____

_____

Mental Exercise: Straighten out the kink so you can effectively do what you were created to do

Have a great week on purpose!

WEEK 48:

GetItStraight

Weekly Affirmation: **I am more than enough. I am worthy. I have a purpose. I make good choices. I choose to be better. I am better. I choose to have a great week on purpose!**

One of the most frustrating things is having a kink in a hose. You go to rinse the car, water your plants, etc., and you get little drops of water or none at all. You then have to go to the place of the kink and straighten it out, so the water flow will no longer be restricted. The hose can then effectively do what it was created to do. How much of our flow is restricted by a kink in our life?

Mental Exercise: Straighten out the kink so you can effectively do what you were created to do.

Have a great week on purpose!

Soul-Search Saturday:

Glow(s):

_____

_____

_____

Grow(s)

_____

Next Steps:

_____

WEEK 49:

Shift

Weekly Affirmation: **I am more than enough. I am worthy. I have a purpose. I make good choices. I choose to be better. I am better. I choose to have a great week on purpose!**

Think about when you're driving and see a "lane closed ahead" sign. Some drivers go ahead and shift lanes, and then there are others who wait until the last minute to try and get over. Oftentimes, they end up stuck for a moment because no one is willing to let them over (maybe that's just Atlanta though, lol). My question is, do you make the necessary shifts in life, or do you wait until the last minute and get stuck?

Mental Exercise: Identify the areas in life where you need to shift your mindset, behavior, attitude, etc.

Have a great week on purpose!

Soul-Search Saturday:

Glow(s):

_____

_____

_____

Grow(s)

_____

_____

_____

Next Steps:

_____

_____

_____

WEEK 50:

PayAttention

Weekly Affirmation: **I am more than enough. I am worthy. I have a purpose. I make good choices. I choose to be better. I am better. I choose to have a great week on purpose!**

Whenever I ride past the airport in Atlanta, GA, I start thinking about the signs and how they direct us where to go. These signs provide direction based on what we are trying to accomplish and/or how we are traveling. If you're not careful though, you'll find yourself driving in circles. Similarly, if we aren't mindful of the signs in our life, we may find ourselves going in circles. Just as at the airport, this can take up time and be frustrating. We must slow down and take our time to look at the signs around us.

Mental Exercise: Pay attention to the signs in life. They will provide direction.

Have a great week on purpose!

Soul-Search Saturday:

Glow(s):

_____

_____

_____

Grow(s)

_____

Next Steps:

WEEK 51:

OneTime

Weekly Affirmation: **I am more than enough. I am worthy. I have a purpose. I make good choices. I choose to be better. I am better. I choose to have a great week on purpose!**

If you're reading this, take a moment to just breathe. There's a lot coming at you from so many directions. It feels like you are playing an opponent that you never beat. It feels like the odds are stacked against you. It feels like no one expects you to win. Sound about right? I know it's tough, and you feel alone. You may even feel defeated, but you cannot afford to have a defeated mentality. Have your moment, but know that feelings are finicky. Don't let them rule you. Keep that winning mentality because a loss is just a lesson learned. There's a scene in one of my favorite movies, *Little Giants*, when the coach is talking to his team about a tough opponent. The team doesn't think they'll win the game, and they're already defeated before the game begins. The coach talks about even if that team beat them 99 times, there's still one time that it could be different. I know we have so many opponents in life, and even if they beat us 99 times out of 100...that still leaves one time. Want to know the secret to smiling through it all? Live in the expectation of that one time.

Mental Exercise: What if today is that one time? Just what if?

Have a great week on purpose!

Soul-Search Saturday:

Glow(s):

_____

_____

Grow(s):

_____

_____

_____

Next Steps:

_____

_____

_____

_____

WEEK 52:

BlindSpots

Weekly Affirmation: **I am more than enough. I am worthy. I have a purpose. I make good choices. I choose to be better. I am better. I choose to have a great week on purpose!**

I can remember several years ago when I was trying to change lanes and collided with another car. Thankfully it wasn't a major accident, more like a bumper car type situation. I didn't collide because I was distracted. I collided because I didn't even see the car coming up beside me, better known as my blind spot. As a result of that accident, I purchased some blind spot mirrors.

As a matter of fact, when I got a new car a few years back, I put some on there too. I needed to feel certain that I could see all things coming up on my blind spots. Some people do fine without them, which is cool; I just feel better with them. For me, why guess when I can be sure?

I want to pose a few questions to you this week. We all have blind spots, but do you have blind spot mirrors on your team? Do you have people who look out for the people and situations you don't see? How many personal and professional collisions could have been avoided if you just had those blind spot mirrors?

Mental Exercise: Identify your personal and professional blind spot mirrors.

Have a great week on purpose!

Soul-Search Saturday:

Glow(s):

_____

_____

_____

Grow(s)

_____

_____

_____

Next Steps:

_____

_____

_____

I hope you've enjoyed this first volume of Monday motivations and have been blessed. Remember, your Mondays are possible!!! ☺

~Daws

About the Author

Ashley D. Dawson is an only child, born and raised in Georgia. She always had a passion for helping and serving others which is a recurring theme in her personal and professional life. She has worked in various capacities such as nonprofits, education, and business. Ashley is the author of *Surviving Your Own Jungle* and *Birthing Pains: Push to the Promises of God*. She's also a co-author of *Girl Power Uncensored*. Ashley enjoys writing, cooking, traveling, and creating. Ashley is a proud member of Alpha Kappa Alpha Sorority, Incorporated and currently resides in Georgia.

Her life's motto: Serve. Inspire. Uplift

Contact Ashley

For book signings and speaking engagements, you can reach Ashley D. Dawson at:

Email: <u>dawsladyllc@gmail.com</u>

Follow her on social media:

Instagram: dawsladyllc_

Website: <u>www.dawslady.com</u>